NEAR WATER

34889708 3/07

Books in the
WATCH OUT! Series:

WATCH OUT! Around Town
WATCH OUT! At Home
WATCH OUT! Near Water
WATCH OUT! On the Road

First Edition for the United States and Canada published in 2006
by Barron's Educational Series, Inc.

Text copyright © Claire Llewellyn 2006
Illustrations copyright © Mike Gordon 2006

Published by Hodder Children's Books in 2006

All inquiries should be addressed to:
Barron's Educational Series, Inc.
250 Wireless Boulevard
Hauppauge, New York 11788
www.barronseduc.com

International Standard Book No. 13: 978-0-7641-3327-5
International Standard Book No. 10: 0-7641-3327-6

Library of Congress Catalog Card No. 2005926318

Printed in China
9 8 7 6 5 4 3 2 1

WATCH OUT!
NEAR WATER

Written by Claire Llewellyn
Illustrated by Mike Gordon

BARRON'S

Do you like playing in the bath,

splashing through puddles,

Here I come!

or jumping in the swimming pool?

Then you'll know
that water can
be lots of fun.

5

But have you ever fallen underwater, lost your breath, and nearly drowned?

Then you'll know that water can be frightening, too.

Some animals can breathe underwater... or hold their breath for a very long time.

Turtl

But people can't.
Underwater, they stop breathing
and after a minute or two they die.

This makes water very
dangerous indeed.

We all need to be careful with water.
Where is the water in your home?

Is there water in the yard?

Do you sometimes go to the swimming pool?

It's important to learn how to swim – though it can take a little time.

Week by week you get a little bit better, and then suddenly...

What could happen if you jumped on your friends or pushed them into the water?

In the summer it's fun to swim in the ocean. Is this like swimming in a pool?

The ocean is strong, and
it is always moving.

It can drag things out to deep water.
It could carry you away.

Some beaches are safer than others. They have flags to show where it is safe to swim and lifeguards to watch over people.

But even so, you must take care
and never ever swim alone.

In the summer, if the ocean is far away, you can go to a river or lake.

You can fish...

...or splash,

or take a boat
out on the water.

21

But the weather can quickly change. One moment, everything is fine.

Then, suddenly, the sky clouds over...

and a wind begins to blow.
Now the water is very choppy.

Rivers and lakes are cold and deep.

If something went wrong, and you fell into the water, it would be very hard to swim.

A life jacket helps to keep you afloat while someone rescues you.

What would happen if you didn't wear one?

25

Take extra care when
you're near a river.

Many rivers are deep and fast moving.

Do you think they're a good place to swim?

Everyone enjoys playing with water.

Most of the time water is fun,
but it can be dangerous too.

Notes for parents and teachers

Watch Out!

There are four titles currently in the *Watch Out!* series: *On the Road, Near Water, At Home,* and *Around Town.* These books will prompt young readers to think about safety concerns both inside and outside the home, while traveling in a car, and even while on a trip or enjoying the outdoors. The lessons illustrated in all four books will help children identify important safety issues and potentially dangerous situations that they may come across in their everyday lives. Gaining the ability to recognize potential dangers—as well as being instructed on how to avoid these hazards—will allow readers to be more aware of the world around them. Whether at home, at a park, by the pool, or on a road trip, this series offers helpful tips and information on a number of common, everyday scenarios children should *watch out* for.

Issues raised in the book

Watch Out! Near Water is intended to be an enjoyable book that discusses the importance of safety in and around water. Throughout, children are given the opportunity to think independently about taking care of themselves and about what might happen if they do not pay attention to safety issues. It allows them time to explore these issues and discuss them with their family, class, and school. It encourages them to think about safety first and about the responsibility and practical steps they can take to keep themselves safe.

The book looks at the things we do in and near water, including baths, garden ponds, swimming pools, lakes, rivers, and the beach. It explains the potential danger of water and asks questions about how children feel about water, and what might happen if someone falls in.

It is also full of situations that children and adults will have encountered. It allows a child to ask and answer questions on a one-to-one basis with you. How does it feel to be splashed by water? How does it feel to fall in water? Have they ever been frightened in this way? Are they learning to swim? How do they feel about going in the ocean? The illustrations provide amusing and helpful ideas.

Being safe in or near water is important for everyone. This book tackles many issues. It uses open-ended questions to encourage children to think for themselves about the consequences of their behavior.

Suggestions for follow-up activities

Think of animals that live in ponds, rivers, and in the ocean. Which ones can breathe underwater? Draw a picture of one or two of these.

What sort of things sink and float? Make a collection of objects and see if they will float in a bowl of water. How do people stay afloat in the swimming pool if they cannot swim?

Draw a picture of a beach on a summer's day. Add a lifeguard and some flags to the beach to show where it is safe to swim.

www.safekids.org—Safe Kids is a national campaign designed to help protect kids from accidents through education. The Web site contains information about various threats to children, product recalls, and research findings.

Books to read

Boelts, Maribeth. *A Kid's Guide to Staying Safe Around Water (The Kid's Library of Personal Safety)*. PowerKids, 1997.

Jackson, Mike. *Look Out by Water*. Evans Brothers Limited, 1994.

Leonard, Stew, and Dr. Lawrence Shapiro. *Stewie the Duck Learns to Swim*. Kimberly Press, 2002.
Stewie the Duck encourages children to learn to swim through song.

Pendziwol, Jean. *A Treasure at Sea for Dragon and Me: Water Safety for Kids (and Dragons)*. Kids Can Press, 2005.
Water safety saves the life of a careless, playful dragon.

Raatma, Lucia. *Safety at the Swimming Pool (Safety First)*. Capstone Press Incorporated, 1999.
Discusses the importance of obeying lifeguards as well as using a buddy system while at the pool.